Democracy – the citizen decide

The United Kingdom is a **democracy**. The word democracy comes from two Greek words, which together mean 'people power'. A democracy is a system of government that involves all the citizens sharing power.

Athens – the birthplace of democracy GkY

Democracy originated in the Greek city of Athens. It was first practised two and a half thousand years ago. In Athens, male citizens gathered together on one of the hills of the city. They did this about 40 times a year. This was called the 'people's assembly'. Here, male citizens had the right to speak – and vote – on important issues.

This system is known as direct democracy: decisions are taken directly by the people themselves. This worked in Athens because the assembly place was big enough to accommodate the 6000 citizens entitled to vote. These citizens regularly played a part in decision-making.

However, the system was not completely democratic. Women, children and foreigners were not allowed to vote. And there were many thousands of slaves in Athens who couldn't vote either.

The speaker's platform on the Pnyx, the hill where the citizens of Athens held meetings

Representative democracy

Direct democracy is a very fair system, but it is impractical for day-to-day government in the UK. There are about 60 million people living in the UK. Every day the government takes thousands of decisions. There is no way that everyone could discuss, debate, and then vote on all of these decisions.

In the UK, a system called **representative democracy** has developed. This is a system of democracy used across much of the world today. In a representative democracy, people elect representatives to make decisions on their behalf. These representatives, or politicians, meet together in a parliament. Because ordinary people are represented by others, this system is called **indirect democracy**.

D[emocracy in] Britain

The government has started to use **referenda** for some decisions. A **referendum** is when all the people vote to decide an issue. Referenda were held to decide whether to set up the Scottish Parliament, and the Northern Ireland and Welsh Assemblies. A series of local referenda have been held across England. These were to decide whether some towns should have directly elected mayors (see page 25). A national referendum will decide whether or not Britain joins the single European currency (see page 29).

Campaigners celebrate winning the right to hold a referendum to decide if Oxford should have a directly elected mayor

(see page 25). ... (see page 29).

Discuss

Imagine that you were setting up a school council. This would control the running of your school. Which system would you choose?

a) A direct democracy, where all students, teachers and parents could meet to make decisions.

b) A representative democracy, where students and teachers elect representatives to make decisions.

Would you let parents vote? How old would students have to be to vote?

1

Being an MP

What is an MP?

The term **MP** stands for 'Member of Parliament'. MPs are members of the **House of Commons**. When speaking to each other MPs use their **constituency** names. For example, David Rendel MP represents the constituency (or area) of Newbury. He is therefore addressed in the House of Commons as 'the Honourable Member for Newbury'.

MPs come from all areas of the United Kingdom – England, Northern Ireland, Scotland and Wales. They usually live in their own constituencies. They also receive an allowance to have a small flat in London. This is because it is difficult for MPs who live a long way away to travel home from London each day.

MPs are paid about £55 000 per year. They also receive an allowance of about £62 000 per year for research staff and secretaries in their constituencies and in the House of Commons.

An MP's diary

David Rendel's Diary

Last Friday in Cold Ash there was a very well attended meeting about traffic. Many more heavy lorries are now using the village as a short cut. On a national level I have called for speeding fines to be used to provide additional speed cameras.

This Saturday my advice surgery was in Thatcham. I like to hold my surgeries in different places so that local people can get to them easily. The big local issue this week has been the Watermill Theatre. Having attended many excellent performances there, I have gladly lobbied the government on their behalf with both letters and questions in the House of Commons.

Monday afternoon began with a meeting of all the Berkshire MPs, to discuss how best to oppose the Government's proposals for green field development in our area. By working together, we hope to achieve some significant reductions.

Peter Mandelson visits his constituents

Whose interests should MPs vote for?

In Parliament MPs have to vote on the many issues being discussed. When voting, MPs are under pressure from many people with different interests. In addition to considering all these different interests, some MPs take on other jobs. These include directorships of companies, or acting as consultants. Some members of the Labour Party are sponsored by **trade unions** to represent their interests.

Supporters of MPs having outside interests claim that they give MPs a wider range of knowledge. This means that they can make better decisions. However, critics argue that the job of an MP should be full-time. These critics say MPs should be banned from taking on other forms of work while they are in Parliament. This is so that they can concentrate on parliamentary business.

Discuss

1 Do you think MPs should be allowed to take on other jobs while they are in Parliament? Give reasons for your views.

2 Read the extract from the column that MP David Rendel writes in a local paper. What do you learn from it about an MP's work both in Parliament and their constituency?

3 Imagine you are an MP. Rank the following in the order which you feel is most important:
  ● local interest
  ● regional interest
  ● national interest
  ● personal feelings
  ● party policy.

4 Imagine you are a representative on a council running your school. Whose interests would be most important to you: parents, teachers, the head teacher or students? Why?

Parliamentary government – the UK system

What makes up a government?

Any government consists of three important parts – the executive, the legislature and the judiciary. The **legislature** makes the laws of the country. The **executive** makes day-to-day decisions, and is responsible for the running of government. Finally, there is the **judiciary**, which interprets the **law**. The judiciary consists of judges and magistrates.

America has a presidential system of government. In this system the head of state is a President, and the legislature, executive and judiciary are independent from each other. This is known as a **separation of powers**.

By contrast, the UK has a parliamentary government. In this system the leader of the largest political party in Parliament becomes the **Prime Minister**, who is the head of the executive. Parliament is made up of the government – MPs of the leading political party – and MPs from other political parties.

Parliament is both a legislative and executive body combined. The UK, therefore, does not have a separation of powers.

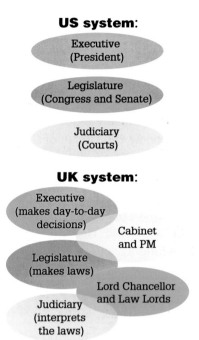

US system:
- Executive (President)
- Legislature (Congress and Senate)
- Judiciary (Courts)

UK system:
- Executive (makes day-to-day decisions)
- Cabinet and PM
- Legislature (makes laws)
- Lord Chancellor and Law Lords
- Judiciary (interprets the laws)

The Cabinet

In the UK, the **Cabinet** is the main executive committee which makes many of the important decisions of government. The Prime Minister appoints 20–25 senior members of his or her party to be ministers in the Cabinet.

There are three top members of the Cabinet:
- The Chancellor of the Exchequer - responsible for all government spending and economic policy
- The Foreign Secretary - responsible for the United Kingdom's relations with other countries
- The Home Secretary - responsible for law and order, the police force and the prison service.

Another member of the Cabinet is the Lord Chancellor. The Lord Chancellor is the Speaker of the House of Lords, and appoints judges. In this way the executive is also linked to the judiciary in the UK.

Another 75-80 members of the government become ministers. These are accountable to members of the Cabinet, and run the country as part of the executive. The monarch, acting on the advice of the Prime Minister, appoints all ministers. It is really the Prime Minister who chooses who to appoint.

The Opposition

Not all MPs support the government. Those MPs from other parties outside of the government form the opposition. The party with the second largest number of MPs forms the Official Opposition. This party's leader is called the Leader of the Opposition. The job of the opposition is to constructively criticize and oppose the government.

The Leader of the Opposition appoints 20–25 MPs to speak on Cabinet matters. These MPs are known as the Shadow Cabinet.

Discuss

1 Do you think having a monarchy is a good idea? Or would it be better if the UK had a President? Give reasons for your views.

2 Do you think we should have a directly-elected cabinet and Prime Minister, which would be separate from Parliament? Give reasons for your views.

The monarch's position

The UK has a head of state called a monarch. However, the monarch does not hold real power. For example, although the monarch has to approve all new laws made by Parliament, in recent times, he or she has never refused to do so.

The powers of the monarch are defined by the United Kingdom's constitution. This is the set of rules and laws distributing power in the state. This is why the United Kingdom is called a **constitutional monarchy**.

Most countries in the world have a written constitution. The UK, however, does not. Instead of being written down in a document, many of these rules and laws are a matter of custom or convention. For example, everybody in the country should be treated as equals. In the UK this right is protected by anti-discrimination laws rather than by being written down in a constitution, as it is in countries such as the USA and France.

Elections

General Elections

An election to choose the members of the House of Commons (MPs) is called a **general election**. A general election has to be held at least once every five years and is held on average every four years.

There are two ways of calling a general election. First, the Prime Minister can call a general election at any time. This is usually when the government is popular because the government hopes to be re-elected.

Secondly, the House of Commons can pass a vote of 'no confidence' in the government. This forces a general election.

In some countries, such as the USA, there are fixed-term elections. This means that the date of the election is set.

Pressure groups such as Charter 88 argue that fixed-term elections are more democratic. This is because no party has control over when an election will be fought.

The candidates

Anyone aged 21 over, who is a UK Citizen on the electoral register (see page 14), can stand as a candidate to become an **MP**. Exceptions include members of the House of Lords, the clergy, judges, civil servants, the police, and those in the armed forces.

Most candidates are nominated by **political parties**.

Some candidates may stand as independent candidates.

Each candidate must deposit £500 with the 'returning officer'. This is the official who is responsible for organizing a fair election. Candidates who fail to get five per cent of the votes cast at a general election lose their deposit.

Campaign finance

Political parties fund their general election campaigns by donations from individuals, businesses, trade unions and other organisations. This has led to allegations that parties have accepted donations in return for favours (see page 22).

In 2001, the Electoral Commission introduced new rules. Political parties may only accept donations above £200 from people on the electoral register, companies that are registered in the UK and trade unions.

In some countries, such as France, public money is used to finance political parties to prevent people from buying political influence. The government has called for a debate, indicating that it would support public finance of political parties only if everyone agrees.

However, the Conservative party is firmly against this and argue that the existing system for funding political practices is sufficient. Public financing of political parties therefore seems unlikely to occur in the near future.

Discuss

Do you think that we ought to have fixed-term elections in the United Kingdom? Why?

Members of the police force are not allowed to become MPs

The Electoral Commission

The Electoral Commission was formed in November 2000. It is independent of any political party.

Powers of the Electoral Commission include:

- responsibility for reviewing electoral boundaries
- monitoring all donations to political parties from all sources, including private individuals, businesses, and trade unions
- overseeing all spending limits for all elections and referenda in the UK
- conducting voting experiments to increase voter turnout (see page 14)
- running campaigns to inform people about elections, and to encourage people to vote.

Discuss

Should we publicly fund political parties or is the money better spent elsewhere? Give reasons for your views.

Who can vote?

Anyone who is 18 or over is allowed to vote in the constituency in which they are living at the time of a general election. There are a few exceptions who are legally disqualified from voting, including members of the House of Lords and convicted prisoners.

How to vote

Each person voting has one vote. Voting is traditionally by secret ballot and takes place at a polling station. Polling stations are usually set up for an election day in church halls, town halls and local primary schools.

Each voter is given a piece of paper called a ballot paper. On the ballot paper is a list of all the candidates' names. The voter puts a cross against the candidate they wish to vote for. They then put the ballot paper in a sealed box, known as a ballot box.

Constituencies

For election purposes, the country is divided into 659 separate areas. These are known as **constituencies**, or seats. All adults who live in a constituency vote to choose one person to represent them in the House of Commons. The idea is that there should be a similar number of people in each constituency.

Not all constituencies have equal numbers of voters living in them. The map shows that the average population size of a constituency in Scotland and Wales is much smaller than constituencies in England.

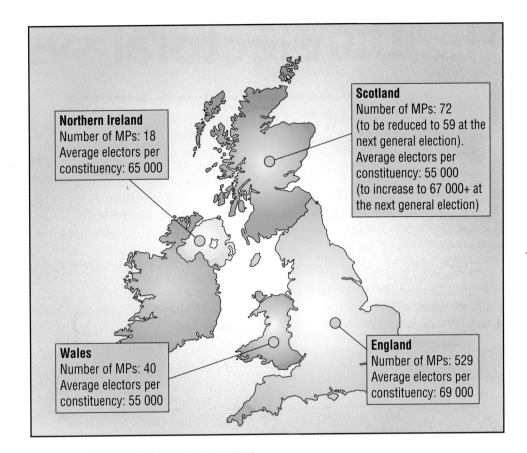

Northern Ireland
Number of MPs: 18
Average electors per constituency: 65 000

Scotland
Number of MPs: 72
(to be reduced to 59 at the next general election).
Average electors per constituency: 55 000
(to increase to 67 000+ at the next general election)

Wales
Number of MPs: 40
Average electors per constituency: 55 000

England
Number of MPs: 529
Average electors per constituency: 69 000

TV and radio

Although allowed in many countries, TV and radio advertising is currently almost completely banned in the United Kingdom. The exception is party political broadcasts, which are broadcast in the evening and must be five minutes long.

In early 2002, the government suggested it might relax the controls on TV advertising, to allow the broadcasting of shorter political adverts.

Discuss

Would you allow political parties to advertise on TV and the radio? If so, should there be limits on the number of adverts they can buy? Why?

Discuss

1 "Now that there is a Welsh Assembly (see page 10), shouldn't the number of MPs for Wales be reduced as well?"

2 You are electing a school's council. Would you allow teachers more votes and more seats than students and parents? Give reasons for your answer.

Proxy and postal votes

Sometimes people are unable to vote in person. For example they may be on holiday on election day. These people can apply for a proxy vote. Voting by proxy means giving another person legal permission to vote for you.

In addition to this, people now have the right to vote by post.

Postal and proxy voting thus help increase turnouts (see page 14).

Campaign spending

There are strict controls on spending for each candidate in each constituency. The Electoral Commission oversees these. The exact amount depends on the number of voters living in the constituency. In total, it allows political parties to each spend up to £20 million in the 12 months before a general election.

However, each candidate is allowed to have one leaflet sent free by the Post Office. This 'freepost' explains the candidate's political views to every voter or household in the constituency.

5

The UK electoral system

First-past-the-post

The current method of voting and counting votes in the United Kingdom is known as 'first-past-the-post'. Each elector has one vote in one constituency. The candidate with the most votes in each **constituency** is elected as an MP.

The system of first-past-the-post has been used in the United Kingdom since 1832. Supporters of this system, including the Conservative Party, argue that it is easy for people to understand. First-past-the-post also means that an MP has a direct link with their constituents (the people who vote for them).

This system also tends to produce decisive results in elections. Generally, one party wins an overall majority, as can be seen in the table below.

Election	% Share of vote	% of seats actually won.
2001	40.7% – Labour	62.51% – 412 seats.
1997	43.2% – Labour	63.4% – 418 seats.
1992	41.9% – Conservative	51.6% – 336 seats.
1987	42.2% – Conservative	57.7% – 375 seats.
1983	42.4% – Conservative	61.1% – 397 seats.

Time for a change?

Pressure groups such as Charter 88 and the Electoral Reform Society have been campaigning to change the electoral system to some form of proportional representation (see page 7). Charter 88 argues that first-past-the-post is unfair because it is not a proportional system. In other words, the number of seats a party wins nationally does not match the number of votes it gets.

In addition to this, the Electoral Reform Society (ERS) argues that first-past-the-post produces many safe seats for political parties. At a general election, only around 100 seats are considered marginal, or likely to change hands. This means that voters in these marginal seats appear to count much more than those voters in safe seats.

Finally, the ERS argues that first-past-the-post leads to many wasted votes. At the 2001 general election the Conservatives won 30% of the votes in West Yorkshire, but no seats. Similarly, Labour polled 22% of the votes in Surrey, but won no seats. Across the country, half of the 659 MPs were elected with less than 50% of the votes in their seat. The ERS claims wasted votes are a major cause of voter apathy (see page 14).

In 2003, after the Scottish and Welsh elections, the Electoral Commission is due to produce a report on electoral reform. Some members of the Labour party are in favour of using the Alternative Vote system (AV). Meanwhile, the Liberal Democrats campaign in favour of the Single Transferable Vote system (STV), while the Conservative party supports first-past-the-post.

The Alternative Vote

Under the Alternative Vote (AV) system, one MP is elected to each constituency, like first-past-the-post. However, instead of voting for one candidate, voters can vote for candidates in order of preference. You would put 1 by your favourite candidate and 2 by your next favourite, and so on.

The winning candidate must get at least 50% of the vote of first preferences. If no single candidate achieves this, the candidate with the least votes is eliminated. Voters' second preferences are then counted and added onto the totals of the first preference votes. This continues until a winner is produced.

The AV+ System

A variation of the AV system is currently used to elect directly elected mayors (see page 25). This is known as AV+. Here, voters are allowed two preferences. If no one candidate wins in the first round, all but the top two candidates are eliminated. Second preferences are then counted and the votes are added onto the original totals. This produces a winner.

Supporters of AV+, including some members of the Labour government, argue that it gives more choice to voters. It also keeps the historic link between an elected official and their constituency. Critics argue that it offers a very limited choice for voters. They add that if AV+ had been used at the 2001 General Election, the government would still have had a large majority, with a minority of votes.

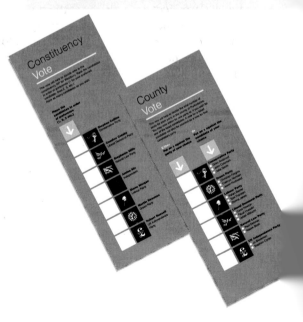

6

Proportional Representation

Proportional Representation (PR) means an electoral system where the number of votes cast for a party roughly equals the number of seats won. Different systems of proportional representation are used in most countries around the world to hold elections, including many of the members of the European Union. Different forms of PR include the Single Transferable Vote and the Additional Member system.

The Single Transferable Vote

The Single Transferable Vote system (STV) is currently used for local, regional and European elections in Northern Ireland. Under STV, voters elect several candidates for one constituency. Like the Alternative Vote, they number the candidates in order of preference. The amount of votes a candidate must get to win depends on the size of the seat.

As the constituencies are shared between several MPs, they tend to be much larger. For example, instead of having one MP in a constituency of 60 000 voters, you would have five or six MPs in a constituency of 300 000.

If STV were introduced in mainland Britain, the major beneficiaries would be the Liberal Democrats and the Scottish and Welsh nationalist parties, at the expense of Labour and the Conservatives.

The Additional Member System

The Additional Member System (AMS) is a mixture of first-past-the-post and regional lists. Under AMS, everyone has two votes – one for a constituency for an individual, and one 'regional' vote, for a registered individual or party. Constituency representatives are elected by first-past-the-post. The regional members are then allocated so that each party's overall share of the seats reflects its regional vote. AMS is used for elections in the Welsh and London Assemblies, and in the Scottish Parliament.

AMS at work in Scotland

The Scottish Parliament has 73 single-member seats, and 56 regional seats split between eight regions. The Scottish National Party only won seven of the constituency seats in the 1999 Scottish elections. However, it was then allocated a further 28 seats because it scored 27 per cent share of the vote against Labour's winning 38 per cent share (with 53 seats). This gave the Scottish National Party 35 seats in the Scottish Parliament, or 27 per cent of the seats.

Regional lists

This system was used in the 1999 elections to the European Parliament in England, Wales and Scotland. Under this system, people vote for parties, not individuals. The country is divided up into different regions – Scotland, Wales, plus the 9 regions of England (see page 11). Each region elected a different number of MEPs, depending on the population of the region. The parties were allocated seats according to their share of the vote in the region.

This was the first time in the UK that voters voted for a party, not an individual. Critics argue that this system gives too much power to parties, who decide what order their candidates are placed on the party lists.

Discuss

1 Do you think that an election system should produce a clear result?

2 Which electoral system do you prefer? Why?

Proportional Representation – for and against

For	Against
● It favours small parties which frequently lose out under first-past-the-post	● PR rarely leads to a result with one clear winner
● PR allows great voter choice by allowing you to list parties in order of preference	● PR weakens the link between an MP and their constituency
● PR works – it allows power sharing in Northern Ireland	● PR leads to backroom deals where parties form coalitions. This takes power away from ordinary voters and gives too much power to small minority parties
● Unless the winning party get over 50 per cent of the vote, it can only form a government with the support of other parties.	● It can be complicated calculating an exact result.

The House of Commons

The Lower Chamber

MPs debating in the House of Commons at **Westminster**, with the government benches to the left, the despatch boxes and the Speaker's chair in the centre and the opposition benches on the right.

Parliament is divided into three parts – the **House of Commons**, the **House of Lords** (see page 12) and the Monarch (see page 3).

The House of Commons is the lower chamber of Parliament. The main function of the House of Commons is to make **laws**. Within this chamber, statements by the government are made to **MPs** so that the House can debate important political issues.

The House of Commons has a calendar year. Like many schools, this is divided into 3 terms. The parliamentary year begins each October or November, and ends in July. There are breaks, known as recesses. These occur every Christmas, Easter and during the summer holidays.

The main business of Parliament is called public business. This includes dealing with the various stages of bills (see page 9). However, on 20 days scattered throughout the year, a debate occurs on a subject chosen by the opposition. These are known as 'opposition days'.

House of Commons sittings

Monday:	2.30pm – 10.00pm
Tuesday, Wednesday:	11.30am – 7.00pm
Thursday:	11.30am – 6.00pm
Friday:	9.30am – 2.30pm

A modern parliament?

Critics of Parliament say the building does not meet the demands of a 21st century building. They argue that because MPs face each other, it makes the House of Commons very confrontational. Some modernizers would like a circular chamber, like the European Parliament. Others would like fewer MPs.

In addition to this, some have criticised the House of Commons because, although it has facilities such as bars and a gym, there is no crèche for MPs to leave their young children.

Meanwhile, new parliament buildings around the world such as the Australian parliament have included a special viewing area solely for school groups. This is so pupils have the chance to watch their MPs at work first hand.

Discuss

1 Imagine you had to design a new layout for the House of Commons. What shape would you make it? What facilities would you include? Why?

2 "The way the House of Commons goes about its business is old-fashioned and needs updating." Discuss this view.

How MPs vote

At the end of a debate, if MPs disagree a formal vote is taken. In order to vote, MPs must be physically present in the House of Commons.

Four MPs from each side of the debate act as tellers, counting the votes. In order for a decision to be made, at least 40 MPs must vote.

To make sure MPs vote, each party appoints several 'whips'. A whip's job is to make sure that MPs of a party turn up and vote, and that MPs vote to support a party's policies. In return, whips listen to MPs views, and pass them back to the party leadership. They also can recommend MPs for promotion to the party leader.

Supporters of the whips argue that without party discipline nothing would get done. Critics of this system argue that it is old-fashioned, and that the whips have too much power. They argue that the House of Commons should have electronic voting, like the European Parliament. Here, MPs would have their own seat with an electronic keypad, which they would use to vote. This would then speed up debates, and allow more legislation to pass through Parliament.

How a law is made

The flow-chart shows how a law is made. A proposal for a new law is called a bill. Bills are usually introduced by the government. A few bills, known as private members' bills, are proposed by individual members of Parliament.

Bills can be introduced in either the House of Commons or the House of Lords. If a bill is started in the House of Commons, it then has to go to the House of Lords, and vice versa. It has to pass through a total of six readings – three readings in each House. If there is disagreement between the two Houses, the Lords can delay a bill (except a financial bill) for up to one year.

The Speaker

The Speaker of the House of Commons is the MPs' chairperson. He or she is responsible for orderly debates within the House of Commons, by ensuring that MPs stick to the rules. In order to speak in the House of Commons, an MP must catch the Speaker's eye. The speaker will then nod at them. It is the custom for the Speaker to invite contributions from the government and the opposition in turn.

Michael Martin, the current Speaker of the House of Commons.

Question time

The first 45 to 50 minutes of a House of Commons meeting is known as Question Time. This is when ministers take it in turn to answer questions about the work of their departments. The most important Question Time occurs at 12pm on Wednesday. This is when the **Prime Minister** answers questions for half an hour.

Supporters of Question Time point out it is important for Parliament to hold ministers to account. Critics argue that it usually becomes a shouting match. This is because both sides of the House of Commons try to score points, rather than engage in real debate.

Parliamentary committees

A large amount of the work of Parliament is done by committees. There are 42 select committees, which examine government business and question government ministers. An example is the Home Affairs Select Committee, which frequently calls the Home Secretary to answer questions on subjects such as how much money is spent on law and order.

Numerous committees are also set up for a limited time to deal with specific issues. These are called standing committees. In 1998, for example, an important standing committee, called the Nolan committee, reported on standards in public life.

Discuss

1 "Prime Minister's Question Time should be longer, with the Speaker given more powers to make sure a proper debate occurs." Do you agree?

2 Propose an alternative system to Question Time, which might be able to eliminate the problems of Question Time.

When a public bill has been drawn up carefully in written form, or *drafted*, it is discussed by the Cabinet.

↓

The bill is then *published*, usually to the House of Commons first. This means that it is printed so that it can be examined – there is no debate at this stage. This is known as the *first reading*.

↓

A few weeks later, the bill has its *second reading* and is debated. A vote is taken, and if a majority approves of the bill, it is passed.

↓

A bill will then go to a *parliamentary committee*, so that amendments (changes) to it can be discussed and made.

↓

The next stage is the *report stage*. The committee sends a report to the House with all of its amendments. These amendments are either approved or changed.

↓

Next the bill receives its *third reading*. Again there is a debate on the bill, and a vote is taken.

↓

Once the House of Commons has approved each bill at all three readings, it is then passed to the House of Lords to go through the same stages as in the House of Commons. If the bill is initially published in the House of Lords it will be debated there first before being passed to the House of Commons.

↓

When it is approved by both Houses a bill is given *royal assent* by a royal commission, representing the monarch. The bill then becomes a law, and comes into force. This is known as an *Act of Parliament*.

Discuss

1 Why do you think a bill has to go through so many stages to become a law? Are so many stages necessary?

2 Imagine you had the chance to propose a new law. What law would you propose? Why?

Regional government

What is devolution?

The word **devolution** means the transfer of power and authority. For centuries the UK was a centralist state, with all the power concentrated at the centre in the Westminster Parliament. Recently, devolution has taken place with the establishment of regional governments for some parts of the United Kingdom.

In 1997 in Scotland and Wales, 1998 in Northern Ireland, and in 2000 in London, the Labour government held referenda to ask the local population if they would like devolution in their area. These areas all voted in favour. As a result, they all now have some sort of regional government.

In May 2002, the government announced it would allow further referenda in England. The next region to vote on devolution will be the North-East of England.

Inside the Scottish Parliament in Edinburgh at its first sitting in 1999

The Welsh Assembly

The devolved body for Wales is called the Welsh Assembly. It has 60 members. Like Scotland, these are elected by the Additional Member System. It is responsible for the same sort of policy areas, including local government, transport and economic development. In May 2002, the Welsh Assembly was also governed by a Labour/Liberal Democrat coalition.

Unlike Scotland, the Welsh Assembly does not have the power to make new laws or change taxes, as the Welsh rejected this option in the 1997 referendum. Instead, it receives a grant from the UK government, which it then decides how to spend. It can also add additional laws onto existing ones – this is called secondary legislation.

Support for the Welsh Assembly has never been strong. In 1997, only 50.3 per cent of people voted for the creation of the assembly, with 49.7 per cent voting against. The Welsh Assembly has made some important changes in policy, such as introducing free prescriptions for people under 25. However, the Welsh Assembly has not been viewed as being as important or as radical as the Scottish Parliament.

The Welsh Nationalist party, Plaid Cymru, who have formed a parliamentary alliance in Westminster with the SNP, also argue that there should be a referendum on independence for Wales.

Rhodri Morgan, First Secretary of the Welsh Assembly

The Scottish Parliament

Since 1998, Scotland has had a parliament in Edinburgh. This parliament has the power to make new laws, and slightly raise or lower taxes from the level set in England. Areas of responsibility include health, education, transport, the environment, social services and housing.

The Scottish Parliament uses a form of proportional representation called the Additional Member System (AMS) to elect its members (see page 8). These are called Members of the Scottish Parliament (MSPs). In May 2002, there were 129 MSPs. Since the Scottish Parliament's first elections in 1998, the Labour party and Liberal Democrats have run Scotland as a coalition government.

Many people in Scotland feel that the new parliament has been a success. In its first 1000 days, the Scottish parliament passed 30 new laws, held 1212 committee meetings and received 480 public petitions. Major decisions have included abolishing the student loans system in Scotland, banning hunting and introducing free places in care homes for the elderly, funded by the taxpayer.

However, critics of the Scottish Parliament say this is not enough. The Scottish Nationalist Party (SNP) argues that the Scottish Parliament could do far more. The SNP adds that Scotland should be independent, so it can speak for itself in international bodies like the European Union and United Nations. The SNP thus argues there should be a referendum on Scottish independence.

Discuss

Should there be independence for Scotland and Wales, or is devolution enough? Give reasons for your views.

The London Mayor

Ken Livingstone, the first Mayor of London.

In May 2000, the Greater London Authority was set up. This contains 25 members elected by the Additional Member system. The main job of the assembly is to hold the directly elected Mayor of London to account.

At the same time, London elected its first directly elected Mayor, Ken Livingstone. This was done using the AV+ system (see page 6).

The Mayor of London oversees the police, fire and emergency services, transport and economic development in the capital.

Northern Ireland

Since 1921, devolution in Northern Ireland has been a controversial issue. In 1998, the Good Friday agreement finally led to the first referendum in both Northern Ireland and in the Irish Republic. This allowed devolution to be set up once again in Northern Ireland.

In May 2002, there were 108 members of the Northern Ireland Assembly, elected by the Single Transferable Vote system (see page 7). The government of Northern Ireland is made up of four parties who share power – the Ulster Unionists, the Democratic Unionists, the SDLP and Sinn Fein (see page 19).

Like the Welsh Assembly, the Northern Ireland Assembly does not make new laws, but receives a grant from the UK government, which it decides how to spend. Law and order remains under the control of the UK government.

Devolution for the rest of England

Since 2000, regional economic policy for the rest of England has been run by Regional Development Agencies. These agencies have no elected members, but are instead accountable to ministers in the government. In May 2002, the government decided to allow further referenda in the English regions on the question of devolution. These new bodies would be assemblies, not parliaments, and would also replace existing county councils (see page 24).

It is proposed that these new assemblies would have power to raise funds by varying the level of council tax in their area. Their responsibilities would include education, social services and regional development.

A BBC opinion poll in March 2002 stated that overall:
● 63 per cent of people in England want regional government
● 72 per cent of people believed that it would give their region a stronger voice in Europe and at Westminster
● 60 per cent thought it would bring government closer to the people, and reduce the democratic deficit (see page 14).

However, in the same poll:
● 62 per cent thought that regional government would just mean more red tape
● 48 per cent thought devolution could just be another 'talking shop' for politicians. This suggests the general public have mixed thoughts about devolution.

Discuss

What powers do you think regional government should have? Should all regional governments have the power to raise taxes? Give reasons for your views.

Opinion Research Business, 1–10 March 2002 for the BBC.

The House of Lords

What is the House of Lords?

The **House of Lords** is the upper chamber of **Parliament**. It assists the **House of Commons** in the governing of the country, but is not as powerful.

The main function of the House of Lords is to examine and revise proposals for new laws. Most bills start in the House of Commons (see pages 8–9) then pass to the House of Lords.

Each year the House of Lords proposes about 2000 amendments to bills. Most of these amendments are accepted by the government and become law.

Sometimes the House of Lords votes against a government proposal. For example, in 2001, it defeated a proposal to ban foxhunting in England and Wales. However, if the House of Lords disagrees with the House of Commons, it can only delay a bill for up to 12 months. Bills concerning public finance cannot be delayed at all.

Like the House of Commons, the House of Lords has its own select committees (see page 9). These can examine legislation and issues in detail. For example, there is a specialist House of Lords committee looking at the issue of genetic cloning of plants and animals.

The House of Lords also acts as the final court of appeal in the British judicial system, and therefore makes the final judgement in legal cases. This is done by the Law Lords.

Lord Irvine, leader of the House of Lords.

Membership of the House of Lords

Currently, membership of the House of Lords is divided up into several different groups:

The Lords Spiritual

The Lords Spiritual include the Archbishops of Canterbury and York and the 24 senior Bishops from the Church of England.

Supporters of keeping the Lords Spiritual argue that it allows Bishops, who are not politicians, an important role. Critics question why one religious group should have special powers, while all others are ignored.

The people's peers

In order to try to increase the number of independent members of the House of Lords, Tony Blair's Labour government introduced the idea of 'people's peers'. Anyone, from any walk of life, could apply to be appointed as a Life Peer.

Over 3000 people applied to become life peers. In April 2001 the first 15 people's peers were appointed. The list proved to be a disappointment. All 15 were from the ranks of the powerful public figures who already dominated membership of the House of Lords.

The Lords Temporal

These consist of:
- The Law Lords. In May 2002 there were 28 Law Lords, who are the most senior judges in the United Kingdom. Three Law Lords usually hear appeal cases. However, up to 12 may hear the most controversial cases. The Law Lords are not affiliated to any particular party.
- Life **Peers**. There are over 560 Life Peers. These are people who have been appointed for life. Life Peers are usually people involved in public life and are often supporters of the particular political party that appoints them.
- Hereditary Peers. Until 1999 there were over 800 Hereditary Peers, who were members of the House of Lords by right of birth. For hundreds of years, the eldest male son inherited his father's place in the House of Lords. In 1999, the first stage of the House of Lords reform was passed and all except 92 Hereditary Peers lost the right to sit in the House of Lords. All of the Hereditary Peers will be abolished in the second stage of the House of Lords reform.

The House of Lords has been criticised for giving an important role to the Archbishop of Canterbury, Dr Rowan Williams, when other religions do not receive equal power.

Discuss

What do you think of the idea of people's peers? What criteria would you use to choose people to appoint as life peers?

Reform of the House of Lords

Do **you** want a House that looks like *this* . . . ?

Charter88

Campaigners from Charter 88, the organization for constitutional reform, protesting against Labour's proposals

In November 2001, the Labour government published its proposals for reform of the House of Lords. The following plan was proposed:

- the abolition of all the remaining hereditary peers
- no new life peers to be created
- the reduction of the House of Lords from 700 to 600 members
- 55% of members to be nominees by political parties (the number appointed by each party to be equivalent to their share of the vote at the last general election)
- 20% to be directly elected
- 20% to be appointed by an independent commission
- 5% 'other' members – 16 bishops and at least 12 Law Lords
- a minimum 30% of the membership should be women.

In addition, it was proposed that the Lords' power to block legislation for a year would be removed. In future, the House of Lords would only be able to delay bills for up to three months.

The government argues that this would preserve the best elements of the old House of Lords, while ensuring the new chamber would be fully representative. Critics argue that if the government won a large majority in the House of Commons, it would gain a majority in the House of Lords. This would mean it would cease in any way to challenge proposed legislation and would merely rubber-stamp it.

An elected house?

In response to the government's ideas, the Conservatives published the following proposal, which has also received support from the Liberal Democrats:

- The House of Lords should keep its power to block legislation for up to one year
- The membership should be reduced by 50% to 300
- It should be re-named 'The Senate'
- 80% (240 members) should be directly elected for 15 year terms by the general public
- 20% (60 members) should be appointed by an independent commission.

Supporters of this plan argue that it is necessary for democracy. In other words, a modern democracy requires an elected second chamber. Critics argue that if this chamber was too democratic it would upstage the House of Commons.

Abolition

Some management consultants have suggested that we should "think the unthinkable" and abolish the House of Lords completely.

In total, there are 115 countries in the world which have only one legislative chamber. This compares with 64 countries which have two chambers in their parliament.

Discuss

How would you reform the House of Lords? Would you make it mostly appointed or mostly elected? Or would you scrap it altogether?

"It is crucial for democracy that the House of Lords keeps its power to block legislation." Do you agree?

A democratic deficit

Is Britain's government democratic?

Some people argue that there is a lack of democracy in Britain's political system. They call this a 'democratic deficit'.

This is because a key element of a democracy is to involve people in making decisions on issues that affect their lives. But many people feel marginalized by the current political system. They take little or no interest in politics and do not bother to vote at elections.

Voter apathy

Voter turnout is the proportion of voters who actually turn out to vote on the day of an election. Turnout is higher in general elections than in local and European elections. However, voter apathy – when people choose not to vote – is a serious problem in the UK. For example, at the 2001 general election the turnout was 59 per cent compared to 72 per cent at the 1997 general election. This was the lowest turnout for over 80 years.

It is suggested that one reason for low turnouts is a lack of proper political debate, partly due to politicians' reliance on spin-doctors to control debates (see page 23).

In response, the government is considering reforms to the electoral system to make it easier for people to vote. Meanwhile, pressure groups campaign to increase political activity among groups under-represented at Westminster. These include women, ethnic minorities and young people.

Tired of the party system?

One reason people give for not voting is that they feel none of the main political parties has anything to offer them. An increasing number of people are choosing to enter politics themselves, either by joining minority parties, standing as independents or joining pressure groups (see page 20). At the 2001 General Election, an independent candidate was elected. More recently, in the 2002 local elections, two independents became the directly elected mayors of Hartlepool and Middlesbrough respectively. Meanwhile, two independent council groups actually took power and now control the councils of Kidderminster and Elmbridge. This trend seems set to rise in the future.

The electoral register

In order to vote, you have to be on the electoral register. This is a list of all the people that can vote in a particular area. To be on the electoral register, you have to be living in the area in the October before the elections occur the next May. You also need to be over 18, and fill out official electoral register forms. This means that homeless people, and people who move house can find it very difficult to vote. In recent years, the number of people not registering has risen. This is especially the case among young people and ethnic minorities.

Giving people more choice

In order to increase voter turnout, the Electoral Commission (see page 4) carried out several voting trials in the 2002 local elections. Experiments to increase voter turnout included the following:

- SMS, or text message voting by mobile phone
- Online internet voting
- Moving polling stations to supermarkets
- All-out postal ballots, where everyone has to vote by post.

However, concerns have been raised about the security surrounding internet and text message voting.

Where all-out postal ballots were held, the turnout rose by 28 per cent. All-out postal voting at a general election would seem likely to significantly increase the turnout. The government is therefore examining whether to introduce all-out postal ballots for all elections.

Another proposal is to move polling day from Thursday to the weekend, when many people have more time.

Discuss

1 What do you think are the causes of voter apathy?

2 Should voting be compulsory, as it is in Australia where you are fined if you do not vote?

Stuart Drummond who became the directly elected mayor of Hartlepool in May 2002. Mr Drummond stood as a joke candidate, dressing up in a monkey suit as H'Angus.

Involving all the people

Young people

Currently you may not vote until you are 18, and may not become an MP until you are 21. In fact, the vast majority of MPs are over 30 and many 18–25 year olds do not bother to vote.

The British Youth Council argues that the needs of young people need urgently addressing if young people of all ages are to feel that their views count. Mock elections have been held in schools to encourage political debate.

Critics have argued that this is merely tinkering at the sidelines. The Liberal Democrats have one drastic solution – to lower the voting age to 16. In May 2002, the government was considering this proposal. Supporters of votes at 16 argue that you already have many adult rights, so why shouldn't you be able to vote?

Critics of voting at 16 argue that 16 is too young. They argue that the voting age should remain at 18, when young people are more mature and have finished their secondary education.

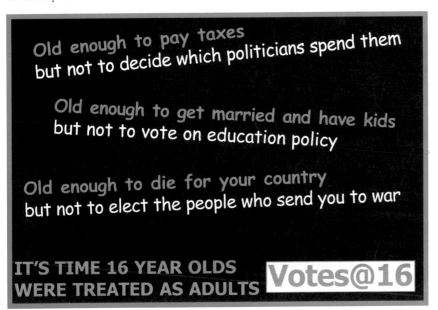

Old enough to pay taxes
but not to decide which politicians spend them

Old enough to get married and have kids
but not to vote on education policy

Old enough to die for your country
but not to elect the people who send you to war

IT'S TIME 16 YEAR OLDS
WERE TREATED AS ADULTS Votes@16

Campaign poster for Votes @ 16

Women in politics

At the 2001 General Election, 115 female MPs were elected. This represents about 17.5 per cent of all MPs. In addition, in July 2001, while there were 720 peers in the House of Lords, only 117 were women (16.25 per cent). The Fawcett Society, which campaigns on women's issues, has called this "a national disgrace".

One way of combating this has been to encourage positive discrimination, through women-only shortlists. This is when a list of only women is drawn up to become candidates to fight a parliamentary seat for a particular political party. When the Labour party did this in 1997 they elected over 100 women. Critics of positive discrimination argue that it is undemocratic, as the best person, whatever their sex, should be chosen for the job.

One other method of increasing the number of women in politics has been to appoint more women when a public appointment is made. Previously, the government stated in 1997 that it would ensure 50 per cent of public appointments went to women by mid-2002. However in May 2002, the figure stood at 34 per cent. The government has changed the target date to 2005.

Operation Black Vote

In May 2002, there were 12 MPs and 24 peers from ethnic minorities. However, seven per cent of the population is from an ethnic minority, a clear case of under-representation.

Operation Black Vote is a pressure group that exists to promote voter turnout among ethnic minorities and campaigns for more ethnic minority MPs to be elected. In 2001, two more ethnic minority MPs were elected. Operation Black Vote points out that "at the current rate of change the House of Commons will become representative in 100 years' time".

Proposals to increase turnout among ethnic minorities have included registration campaigns, positive action to support ethnic minority candidates and electoral reform. While it is now legal to positively discriminate with all women shortlists, this is not the case for ethnic minorities.

Paul Boateng, the new Chief Secretary to the Treasury

Discuss

1 What factors are there which might make it more difficult for a woman to become an MP than for a man? What measures could be introduced to overcome these factors?

2 "How about appointing black people when a public appointment is made? Why should there be a target for women, but not for other minority groups?" Discuss this view.

3 "Young people are just too irresponsible to be allowed to vote at 16. They don't understand political issues." Do you agree or disagree? Give reasons for your answer.

Government Finance

Taxation – how the government raises money

Each year the government has to raise money to finance public spending. Public spending is the money spent on health, social security, housing, defence and many other areas. The government raises this money by setting **taxes**. Taxes can be on a variety of items, for example, on people's incomes, on the goods they buy, or on the profits made by companies.

Each year the government sets out the level of taxes in an economic statement known as the **budget**. The budget is usually made in the spring. The Chancellor of the Exchequer (the member of the Cabinet in charge of government spending) presents the budget in a 'budget statement' to the House of Commons.

The budget also outlines the government's economic objectives and the targets that need to be set in order to achieve these objectives.

The Chancellor, Gordon Brown

Different types of taxes

Some taxes are known as direct taxes. Direct taxes relate directly to the amount that people earn, so that people pay more tax as they earn more money. Income tax is an example of direct taxation. In fact it is the largest source of government revenue: 26% of all government revenue was raised in this way during 2001–2.

Other taxes are known as indirect taxes. These do not relate to the amount that people earn, but stay at a fixed rate. For example, VAT (Value Added Tax) is chargeable on many household goods and services. This means that it is added to the price of a product. The person or business that sells you the product pays the VAT back to the government. The rate of VAT for most goods is 17.5 per cent in the United Kingdom. VAT made up 15 per cent of government revenue in 2001–2.

Finally, there are proportional taxes. A proportional tax stays at exactly the same percentage, whatever you earn. National Insurance (NI) is an example of a proportional tax. This is used to fund social security payments, such as the state pension. NI forms a large part of social security contributions, which were 16 per cent of government revenue in 2001–2.

The sources of government revenue, 2001–2002

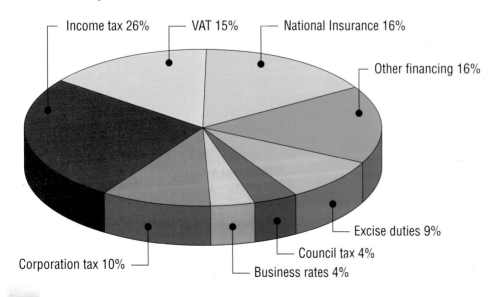

- Income tax 26%
- VAT 15%
- National Insurance 16%
- Other financing 16%
- Excise duties 9%
- Council tax 4%
- Business rates 4%
- Corporation tax 10%

Inflation

One of the targets the government sets in the budget is an inflation target. **Inflation** refers to the amount the prices of goods have gone up over the last year. For example, if houses have risen in price by five per cent over the last year, then inflation for housing will be five per cent.

The government sets inflation targets because of the damage that inflation can do if it gets out of control. If inflation is too high, then the economy 'over-heats'. This means that prices rise too fast and ordinary people suffer because household goods become more and more expensive. However, if inflation is too low, the economy might slow down and go into a recession. In a recession, the economy shrinks rather than grows. This means that people have less money to spend and their jobs are more at risk.

Discuss

Which of the following statements do you agree with most, and why?

a "Direct taxes are fairer than indirect taxes, because people then pay according to the amount they earn."

b "But if direct taxes are too high, they prevent economic growth because people have less money to spend. Also, rich people should not be penalised for their high incomes. They've worked hard to earn the money."

How the government spends money

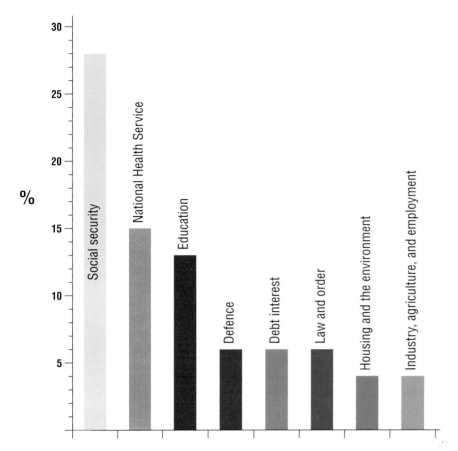

Government expenditure, 2001–2:

UK 2002, by National Statistics, published by HM Stationery Office

Social security

By far the largest area of government expenditure is social security. This covers unemployment benefits, income support and pensions. Together, these accounted for 28 per cent of government spending in 2001-2. The government has taken several steps to reduce this item of expenditure.

First, the government introduced the 'Welfare to Work' scheme. The aim of this scheme is to help more young people to get jobs. The idea was to reduce the amount the government spends on unemployment benefit. Secondly, the government also committed itself to encouraging more private pension schemes, which are funded by the people themselves. This is to reduce spending on state pensions.

Despite this scheme, the UK still faces a massive pensions crisis. Every year the proportion of retired people compared to the proportion of younger, working people is increasing. So there are fewer younger people paying taxes to fund an increasing number of state pensions.

Social security spending fell by four per cent from 1997-8 to 2001-2. However, there are still many young long-term unemployed dependent on benefits. In addition, many people are still not saving enough money to finance their own retirement. If these issues are not addressed soon, the immense strain placed on the social security system may cause it to collapse completely.

Every year, the government also decides how much money it will spend in each government department. There are 15 main departments in the government. These include the Treasury (which controls the budgets of all the departments), the Home Office (law and order), the Foreign Office, Education and Employment, Defence, Social Security and the Department of the Environment.

Public expenditure used to be set out on a yearly basis. However, in 1998 the new Labour government decided to produce a three-year programme of government expenditure. The new budget in 2002 means spending on the National Health Service is set to rise dramatically over the next three years.

Some government expenditure is index-linked. This means that it cannot rise above the rate of inflation.

Private Finance Initiatives

In some cases, the government has introduced private finance initiatives (PFIs). Here, the government sets out the service it requires, and the private sector provides it. For example, the government has asked many private building companies to build new hospitals. Supporters of PFIs argue that this brings in valuable private money to the public sector and creates competition, which in turn should keep costs down. Opponents of PFIs claim that this is privatisation of what should be public services, and that these companies could rip off the government.

Discuss

1 Imagine you were deciding the government's spending programme. What three areas would you allocate the most money to?

2 If you had to take money from other areas to finance your priority projects, where would you take the money from? Would you use a private finance initiative? Why? Give reasons for your views.

Political parties

A **political party** is a collection of people who broadly share the same views. They group together so that they can share their resources and give themselves a better chance of gaining power.

The United Kingdom can be described as having a two-party system. This is because since 1945 the government has either been Labour or Conservative. Between them, these two parties have controlled the vast majority of seats in Parliament. The main reason for this has been the UK electoral system (see page 6).

However, there are signs that the two-party system is weakening. Firstly, voter turnout has been declining steadily since 1945 (see page 14). Secondly, there has been a rise in support for minority parties, including the Liberal Democrats, the SNP and Plaid Cymru.

Also, there are more independent candidates standing for parliament, two of whom have been elected. From 1997–2001, Martin Bell was independent MP for Tatton in North-West England, and in 2001, Dr Richard Taylor became the independent MP for Wyre Forest.

Labour

Leader: Rt. Hon. Tony Blair, Prime Minister
When in power: 1974–79, 1997–present day
Number of MPs at 2001 general election: 412

Prime Minister Tony Blair

Key policies:

- Education: Partnership of the public and private sector. Invest in more classrooms and resources.
- Health service: Dramatically increase resources for the NHS by raising National Insurance. Bring down waiting lists. Reform badly-managed hospitals.
- Europe: Believe in joining the **single currency** when the time is right. British people to be consulted in a referendum.
- Taxation: No increase in income tax. Will raise national insurance and indirect taxes, if necessary.
- Funding: By trade unions and individual membership.

Conservatives

Leader: Rt. Hon. Iain Duncan-Smith
When in power: 1970–74, 1979–1997
Number of MPs at the 2001 general election: 166

Iain Duncan–Smith

Key policies

- Education: Greater role for the private sector. Invest in education, with private finance to support public expenditure.
- Health Service: Create a free market among hospitals to raise standards. Look at experiences from other countries to help reform the NHS.
- Europe: Firmly against a single currency and a federal Europe. Wants Europe to be a collection of nation states that trade with one another.
- Taxation: Advocates tax cuts in the long term.
- Funding: Largely by big business.

LIBERAL DEMOCRATS

Leader: Rt. Hon. Charles Kennedy MP
Number of MPs at 2001 general election: 52

Charles Kennedy

Key policies:

- Education: Invest in education by increasing spending, and giving more power to local councils.
- Health service: Abolish charges for eye and dental tests. Bring down waiting lists.
- Europe: Believes in joining the single currency at the earliest opportunity. British people to be consulted in a referendum.
- Taxation: Reform the tax system to close loopholes that benefit the super-rich.
- Funding: By individual party members.

Scottish and Welsh nationalist parties

The Scottish National Party (SNP)

Leader: John Swinney MP
The Scottish National Party campaigns for an independent Scotland. In 2002, the SNP had five MPs, two Members of the European Parliament (MEPS) and 35 Members of the Scottish Parliament (MSPs). It also controlled three local councils in Scotland.

Plaid Cymru

Leader: Ieuan Wyn Jones
Plaid Cymru means 'the party of Wales' in Welsh. It is also known as the Welsh Nationalist Party. It campaigns for an independent Wales. Since 1992 it has had four MPs at Westminster. In 2002, it had 17 seats in the Welsh Assembly, two MEPS and controlled one local council.

On the fringe

There also exist several small 'fringe' parties in the United Kingdom. These include:

- The Green Party, which campaigns for the protection of the environment. In 2002, the Green Party had two MEPs, three members of the London Assembly and one MSP.
- The United Kingdom Independence Party (UKIP), which campaigns for the UK to withdraw from the European Union. In 2002, it had three MEPs, but no MPs.
- British National Party (BNP), which is a right-wing extremist party. The BNP argues that only white people should run Britain. In 2002, it had three local councillors in Burnley.

Funding

At present, political parties are financed by donations (see page 4). Political parties are restricted in terms of who they are allowed to accept donations from, and all donations are listed at www.electoralcommission.org.uk. This has created a transparent system, to avoid sleaze (see page 22).

In 2002, the Labour Government opened a debate on state funding of political parties. The idea was to give each political party some public money. This would make all political parties more independent financially. It would also make it harder for people outside government to 'buy' power.

Northern Ireland

In Northern Ireland, the political parties are split into three separate groups: Unionists, Republicans and non-sectarian.

On the Unionist side, there exist a number of political parties, firmly committed to Northern Ireland staying in the United Kingdom. These include David Trimble's Ulster Unionist Party with six MPs in Parliament and 28 seats in the Northern Ireland Assembly (see page 11).

There is also the Reverend Ian Paisley's Democratic Unionist Party, with five MPs, and 21 seats in the Northern Ireland Assembly. In addition, there is the Alliance party, which does not have any MPs, but does have six seats in the Northern Ireland Assembly. Another three Unionist parties hold nine seats in the Northern Ireland Assembly between them.

On the Republican side are parties that support a United Ireland. The Social Democratic and Labour Party (SDLP) is led by Mark Durken, with three MPs and 24 members of the Northern Ireland Assembly. There also exists Sinn Fein, the political wing of the IRA, with four MPs and 18 members of the Northern Ireland Assembly. Sinn Fein is led by Gerry Adams.

Finally, there is the non-sectarian Women's coalition, which has two members of the Northern Ireland Assembly. It is neutral, and simply campaigns for an end to the violence in Northern Ireland.

Discuss

1 Do you think we need political parties? Would it be better to have many more independent MPs?

2 What are the arguments for and against the state funding of political parties?

3 If you were considering joining a political party, which one would you join? Why?

Pressure groups

Influencing the government

A **pressure group** is a group of people who try to influence the government, without actually taking power themselves. Pressure groups are usually concerned with just one issue, or one area of policy.

An example of a 'single-issue' or 'cause' pressure group is The European Movement, which campaigns for the UK to join the single currency (see page 29). This is opposed by Business for Sterling, another single-issue pressure group.

Other pressure groups are 'sectional' pressure groups, which seek to influence a wide area of government policies. The Countryside Alliance, for example, seeks to influence all government policies relating to the countryside.

Since the 1950s, membership of political parties has declined overall. Meanwhile, the number and size of pressure groups has risen rapidly. Today in the United Kingdom, there are a variety of pressure groups, including trade unions, environmental pressure groups and employers' pressure groups. An example of an employers' pressure group is the CBI, the Confederation of British Industry.

Discuss

1 "Members of Greenpeace tearing up crops are just as bad as terrorists." Do you agree? Or do you think civil disobedience can sometimes be justified? Give reasons for your views.

2 Imagine you wanted to change a law. Would you form a pressure group, or join a political party? Why?

Pressure group techniques

Lawful pressure

One way pressure groups may seek to influence the government is by **lobbying** politicians (see page 22). Pressure groups may also try to gain favourable media coverage. This can be done in many ways, such as adverts, press releases and media stunts. For this reason, pressure groups often employ their own spin-doctors (see page 23).

One favourite media stunt for pressure groups is to dedicate a particular day or week to a specific cause. For example, the pressure group ASH, Action on Smoking and Health, organises and promotes 'National No-Smokers Day'.

Amnesty International campaigners protesting against the death sentence of Tracy Housel

Unlawful pressure

Sometimes pressure groups use civil disobedience to promote their cause. This is when a person chooses to break the law in a non-violent way. For example, environmental campaigners have destroyed many fields of genetically modified crops.

A few pressure groups break the law by violent protest. One example is the Animal Liberation Front (ALF). The ALF has attacked and firebombed laboratories involved in animal experiments.

There also exist groups, such as the Continuity IRA and al-Qaeda, who both seek to force political change by terrorizing people through murder and violence. Members of such organisations are known as **terrorists**.

Greenpeace activists tear up genetically modified crops, which they consider to be dangerous to the environment

Pressure groups versus political parties

Some pressure groups have been highly successful. Their focus on individual issues can be a powerful force for change. For example, Amnesty International, which campaigns against Human Rights abuses, has over one million members worldwide. It has had many successes. As well as saving thousands of people worldwide from torture and wrongful imprisonment, it has also contributed to the making of legal documents such as the new European Charter of Human Rights.

Some people believe that pressure groups are now more effective than political parties. However, pressure groups can only seek to influence events, and the people who make decisions. By contrast, political parties have a very wide range of interests – and direct experience of controlling power.

Trade unions

One special type of pressure group is a trade union. A trade union is a group of workers in a particular trade, who come together to promote their common interests. Trade unions are therefore a good example of sectional pressure groups.

Trade unions have existed in the United Kingdom since the early 1830s. At one point, it was illegal to be a member of a trade union. This did not last long, however. By the beginning of the twentieth century, trade unions were a major force in British politics, helping to form the Labour Party in 1900.

Today, there exists a federation of trade unions, known as the Trades Union Congress (TUC). Despite reforms in the 1990s, the TUC is still linked closely with the Labour Party to such an extent that it even has a say in the running of the Labour Party.

Leading trade unionists at the annual Trades Union Congress (TUC) meeting

Discuss

1 Do you think trade unions serve a useful purpose? Would you want to join a trade union, or would you prefer not to be a member? Why?

2 Do you think that a party of government should be influenced by the trade unions?

Trade unions in action

During their history, trade unions have used a wide range of techniques to achieve their aims. Apart from lawful pressure that all pressure groups can use, trade unions also use the power of their workers. This can include striking, when workers refuse to work until their demands are met. Members of a trade union can also 'work to rule', which means that they refuse to do any additional work not in their job descriptions.

Trade unions also co-operate more constructively with their employers to achieve their aims. This can include representatives of trade unions meeting with the managers of a company to discuss issues of pay and conditions of work. Trade unions often produce reports on the health of their workers, and on other working conditions. Finally, like many pressure groups, trade unions may also lobby government on legislation and government decisions that affect them.

TUC warns of strikes over pensions crisis

Britain's employers were put on alert yesterday that employees were increasingly prepared to take industrial action to defend their pensions, now the single most important issue at work.

The moderate leader of Britain's 7 million trade unionists declared himself a "militant" over pensions and backed strikes as a means of preventing cuts in payments. John Monks, the general secretary of the Trades Union Congress (TUC), said he was engaged in a campaign to "wake up Britain" to the fact that workers were being betrayed by employers and were now suffering a pensions crisis.

Roger Lyons, the joint leader of Amicus, a union for skilled manufacturing staff, said the TUC would be "drawing a line in the sand" on the issue. Speaking on the eve of the annual TUC conference in Blackpool, he said nine out 10 Amicus representatives would support strike action to defend pensions.

Mr Monks said that corporate Britain should be "hanging its head in shame" on the issue. He added: "Some people like to divide trade unions into moderates and militants. Let me tell you, we're all militants when it comes to defending and advancing pension rights."

As militancy grew among unions, the Confederation of British Industry revealed that in a survey of 940 firms, 225 had already shut their final salary pension schemes, which guarantee retirement payments, and 113 were considering doing so.

Bill Morris, leader of the largest union, the Transport and General Workers Union

Adapted from The Independent, 9 September 2002

Lobbyists

What is lobbying?

Farmers lobby parliament during the 2001 Foot and Mouth Crisis

A **lobbyist** is a professional who tries to influence government decisions. This is known as **lobbying**. Usually this is on behalf of a **pressure group**, a company or a particular industry, known as a client. In the past few years, local government councils have hired lobbyists to influence central government on important decisions that will affect them.

The term 'lobby' comes from an area known as the central lobby within the Houses of Parliament. This is where MPs meet people who wish to argue their views to parliament. Individual constituents may also meet their particular MP here to express their concerns.

Cash for access?

In recent years, the role of lobbyists has increasingly been questioned. This is because individuals have been able to get government decisions that benefit them in return for donations and political favours. All three major political parties have been involved.

Critics of the lobbying system argue that decision-making needs to be more transparent, so that everyone can see what is going on. This has led the government to consider the state funding of political parties (see page 4).

However, supporters of the lobbying system argue lobbying does a lot of good. It allows pressure groups, companies and trade unions to express their concerns to government. This often results in helpful amendments to government legislation.

Many MPs legitimately work for companies, trade unions or pressure groups, and lobby on their behalf. In order to prevent any conflicts of interest, a public register is kept called the 'Register of Members' Interests' and details which organisations an MP works for. It is available on the internet at www.parliament.the-stationery-office.co.uk.

The Hinduja brothers were accused of obtaining British passports, in return for a donation towards the government costs of part of the Millennium Dome.

Discuss

1 Imagine you were drawing up a code of conduct for lobbyists. What rules would you include to make lobbying fair?

2 Do you agree that lobbyists should be restricted to introducing clients to specific politicians?

Firms of lobbyists

In Westminster, there are many firms of political lobbyists. These include companies such as GPC Market Access, Lawson Lucas Mendelssohn and Westminster Strategy. Each claims that they can help their clients to influence government decisions. They do this in several ways:

● by providing advice on who to meet
● by arranging meetings between clients and MPs, Lords or ministers
● by drawing up strategies that influence government decisions.

Lobbying companies usually have a variety of political staff working for them. In this way, their connections throughout all the main political parties are as wide as possible. This gives the company more power to influence decisions.

How the lobbying system works:

Lobbying company meets client and draws up strategy for influencing a decision.

Specific MPs, ministers and Lords are identified, who may be able to help.

Lobbying company either arranges meetings between client and politicians; or meets politicians themselves to lobby on client's behalf.

Decisions are then influenced.

Spin doctors

Giving a spin

A **spin doctor** is a person who tries to manipulate the media. This is achieved by telling a story in a particular way, or by promoting one part of a story. It is done so that the person or party appears in the best possible light. This is known as giving the story 'a spin'.

The term 'spin doctor' originated in America from the spin put on a ball to deceive an opponent in baseball. During the late 1980s, the term crossed over the Atlantic, and is now widely used in politics in the United Kingdom.

Who are the spin doctors?

Today, spin doctors are employed by a variety of groups. Some spin doctors, like Alastair Campbell, work for the government, and are thus civil servants. Other spin doctors work for political parties and pressure groups or public relation departments within large companies.

All senior members of the government have special advisers, who are usually spin doctors. Some political commentators argued that the low voter turnout in the 2001 general election was due to government spin doctors stifling debate, and controlling the news agenda. This emphasizes the power of the media.

Even the Royal Family has its own spin doctors. It was a spin doctor who masterminded the coverage of the Queen Mother's funeral in early 2002, ensuring that the Royal Family got the best possible media coverage.

Spin doctors use a variety of techniques to manage the media. These include:
- leaking information and controlling what information is released
- drawing more or less attention to a news story
- giving anonymous briefings, that is, giving journalists information 'off the record'
- choosing when to release a news story, and in what manner.

These techniques can be 'positive' or 'negative' (see below).

A controversial trade

Spin doctors wield a large amount of power on politicians' behalf. Some people argue that they are too powerful. This is because spin doctors are unaccountable; they have no public responsibility. They also do not operate openly.

Criticism has been made when spin doctors make statements to the media, where they are not identified. These are often reported in newspapers as "senior sources within the government" or "sources close to the leader of the opposition".

Supporters of spin doctors argue that they are there to co-ordinate government policy. Also, they argue that the system allows more information and opinions to be reported to the general public.

One place this occurs is the parliamentary lobby, an area in Westminster where journalists are briefed each day by the government's spin doctors. This allows journalists to question closely the workings of government.

Labour's foremost spin doctor, Alastair Campbell with Tony Blair

Spin doctoring – two case studies

Positive Spin

The day after the budget in April 2002, the Health Secretary made a series of major announcements, detailing a massive growth in funding for the NHS. The government was careful to make sure there were no other major government announcements that day. This is an example of positive 'spin doctoring', to give a story maximum coverage. Here the government created a 'slow news day', where there is little news to report.

Negative Spin

On September 11 2001, the news was dominated by events in New York City. A government spin doctor sent a memo to a colleague, recommending the government should release any bad news it had. This was so that nobody would notice the bad news, because everyone would be concentrating on the terrorist attacks. The attacks had made it a 'fast news day', where there was a lot of news to report. This was judged to be an example of negative spin 'gone too far'.

Discuss

1 How far do you think spin doctors should be allowed to influence the media?

2 Do you think it is right that spin doctors can brief the media anonymously?

Local government

The purpose of local government is to allow people some control over local issues, such as education in local schools, local housing and leisure facilities.

In recent years, there has been a decline in the power of local government. In the 1980s, the Conservative government transferred many of the powers of local government to central government in Westminster, and outside agencies. In 2002, the Labour government was considering proposals to transfer many planning powers concerning controversial developments to the Department of the Environment at Westminster.

How local government is organised

Until the 1990s, most local government across the UK was organised as a two-tier system. The highest level was the **county council** or regional council. Each county council was then divided into a number of local districts (run by **district councils**), reporting to their county council. Parish and town councils also existed at a lower level in most areas.

In Scotland, Wales and Northern Ireland, the two-tier system was eventually replaced by a system of unitary authorities with one level of local government.

In England many areas chose to keep the two-tier system. England therefore has a mixture of one and two-tier local government.

Councils provide a range of services including refuse and recycling collection.

One-tier bodies

Unitary authorities and metropolitan councils

A **unitary authority** means there is only one level of local government. They exist across the whole of Scotland, Wales and Northern Ireland, and there are 46 unitary authorities in England. Unitary authorities are responsible for all local services. In areas around major cities, such as Manchester, there are metropolitan councils. They are called either metropolitan district councils or metropolitan borough councils, and are responsible for all local services.

Discuss

1 What system of local government does your local area have?

2 Imagine you were setting up a system of local government.

● Would one or two levels be better?
● What policy areas would it be responsible for (health, education, etc.)?
● Would you have a local cabinet?

Give reasons for your answers.

Two-tier bodies

County councils

County councils are the highest level of local government in two-tier areas. County councils exist across most parts of rural England. They are responsible for education, social services and local transport. Elections occur for county councils every four years.

District councils

This is the lower level of local government in two-tier systems. They are responsible for refuse collection, housing and leisure facilities. District council elections either occur once every four years, or by thirds. This means that the council elects a third of its members every three out of four years.

Town and parish councils

Town and parish councils also exist in most areas. These have very limited powers, looking after town halls and museums, and coordinating twinning visits with other towns. These councils are often not party political, but are run by independent local residents.

Local cabinets

In 2001, the government decided to reform the structure of local government. Instead of havin many committees, local councils would now be run by one executive committee – either a loca cabinet, or a directly elected mayor (see page 25). This would operate similarly to the Cabinet in central government (see page 3).

The government argues that this system would be more efficient, leading to better decision-making. Critics argue that this reduces local democracy by taking power away from ordinary local councillors.

Financing local government

Most of the funding for local councils comes from central government. The rest is collected by district councils or unitary authorities. This includes local business rates, which are taxes paid by local businesses. These **tax** rates are proportional to the value of the premises the businesses occupy.

Local councils also collect the council tax, which is paid by households. The amount you pay in council tax is dependent on how much your house is worth. The idea is that the size of a person's house is related to their income. The level of council tax is determined by local councils, subject to central government approval.

Critics of this system argue that it does not take into account people's ability to pay. They say that there should be a local income tax to finance local government. This would be directly linked to the amount a person earns. Similarly, it is argued that business rates should be determined by the amount a company earns, not by the size of its premises.

Discuss

1 Do you believe that local government should be financed by a local income tax or a council tax?

2 Should local councils be allowed to set this level of tax independently?

Local councillors

Representatives of local government are called councillors. Anyone can stand for the local council, provided they are over 21, and either live in the local area, or are employed or own a business there. However, you cannot become a local councillor if you work for the local council, are seriously mentally ill, or have been declared bankrupt in the last five years.

When they take decisions, local councillors have to balance the interests of local constituents, the regional interest, the national interest, personal feelings and party loyalties. For example, there might be a proposal to build a new waste incinerator, which would create new jobs, but damage the local environment.

Amateurs and professionals

Most local **councillors** are volunteers. Although many are unpaid, they do receive attendance allowances for going to meetings, as well as travel allowances.

Local councillors are also allowed some time off from their work to attend meetings. Whereas district councils often meet in the evening, county councils and unitary authorities meet in the day. This means that the type of people attracted to be councillors are often those who own their own businesses or who have part-time jobs.

Recently, a small number of local councils have considered paying their members in order to ensure that they do their job properly. For example, in Hackney, a London metropolitan council, the mayor is paid a salary of £17000.

Directly elected mayors

In 2002 local towns and cities were also allowed to hold referenda to decide whether or not to have a directly elected mayor. This would replace the current system, where local councillors elect a mayor each year.

Supporters of this system argue that it is more efficient, as a directly elected mayor would have more power. They also argue it is more democratic, providing a direct link with local voters. Critics of the system argue it undermines the power of local councillors.

Discuss

What do local councillors do? Would you ever volunteer to be a local councillor? Give reasons.

Has your local council made any important decisions affecting the area in the last year? (You may need to contact the council.) Do you approve of those decisions?

Are directly elected mayors a good idea? Should they be paid? Give reasons for your answers.

Councillors debate local issues at a town hall meeting

The European Union

What is the European Union?

The **European Union** is a group of 15 countries that have decided to share power. The main idea of the European Union was to create a common market. In this market, all goods, services and labour can be freely traded across the whole of the European Union.

The EU – a problem or a solution?

All three main political parties support being members of the European Union. They argue that the United Kingdom's trade with other countries has grown massively since the UK joined the European Union.

Supporters of the European Union also add that you can travel freely within EU countries, with few border controls. In addition to this, any citizen of the European Union can:

● work and live freely in any of the 15 member states (countries) without a visa
● vote and stand in local government elections in their country of residence
● be protected by representatives of any member state in any country in the world if their own country is not represented.

Critics argue that the European Union is inefficient. This is because money is sometimes lost because of corruption at local levels within some EU member states. Groups such as the United Kingdom Independence Party (UKIP) argue that the UK would be better off leaving the European Union. They would prefer to trade more with the USA and the countries of the Commonwealth (see page 30).

Critics also claim that many European institutions such as the European Council of Ministers and European Commission (see page 27) are undemocratic because ordinary people are not able to hold them to account. Finally, many opponents of the European Union fear that it undermines the UK's national sovereignty. This is because European law has supremacy over national law.

Is bigger better?

In recent years, over 10 countries have applied to join the European Union. They include many former communist countries from Eastern Europe. Some politicians, including the Prime Minister, are in favour of a larger Europe. They argue that this will lead to a large market for all the companies trading within the European Union. Human rights could then be guaranteed in these countries. It would also mean a larger role for the European Union in world politics.

Critics have argued that enlarging the EU will make it unworkable. The fear is that with too many countries it will be impossible to reach an agreement on anything, without ignoring the wishes of some member countries.

The current structure of the EU

The Council of Ministers

The Council of Ministers is the main decision-making body of the EU. It has one representative from each member country – a minister. Usually the Foreign Secretary attends from the UK, but it depends on what subject is being discussed. For example, if the Council of Ministers is discussing food safety, then the minister responsible for agriculture will attend.

Decisions of the Council are usually passed by a majority. This is known as majority voting. However, in a few crucial areas, such as tax rates, any one government can block a proposal. This is known as the national veto.

The European Commission

The Commission, based in Brussels, has three major roles. Firstly it proposes policies and drafts laws. Secondly, it ensures that EU treaties and other measures are implemented by member states. Finally, it oversees the administration of the EU.

The Commission has 20 commissioners. One commissioner is appointed per country, except for France, Italy, Germany, the UK and Spain, which have two commissioners because they have larger populations to represent. The commissioners are appointed by the governments of their member country. However, they are supposed to act independently of their own government. Each commissioner oversees an area of policy.

Two or three times a year, government heads meet in the European Council to discuss broad matters of policy. Each member state has the presidency of the council for a six-month period.

The European Court of Justice

The European Court of Justice sits in Luxembourg. It has 15 judges, one from each member country. The court resolves disputes about European Union laws, and clarifies the scope and meaning of EU laws. It has the power to rule against national governments.

The European Parliament

The European Parliament is the only directly elected body in the European Union. It has 626 members, known as **MEPs**. Elections are held every five years. In 1999, proportional representation was used for the first time in the UK's European elections. The next elections to the European Parliament are in 2004 and 2009.

The main function of the European Parliament is to discuss proposals put forward by the Commission. It does this in standing committees, which then report to the full European Parliament for debate. The Parliament gives its own opinions. It may make some amendments to the Council's proposals, but its decisions are not binding. The European Parliament also enforces European Union regulations.

How European laws are made

- The Commission sends a proposal for a new EU law to the European Parliament.
- The European Parliament discusses it, and perhaps amends it. It then passes it back to the Commission.
- The Commission drafts a firm proposal, which is sent to the European Council.
- The Council makes suggestions and amendments, consulting its national parliaments. It then adopts a common position on the proposal.
- The common position is considered by the European Parliament. If the European Parliament approves, the Council adopts the proposal. Even if the Parliament rejects, the Council can adopt the proposal as long as it is unanimous.
- EU regulations automatically become law in all member states. The EU can also pass directives that tell member states to introduce a new law within a time limit.

Discuss

1 Where do you think the majority of the power lies in the European Union?

2 'The UK should lose the national veto because majority voting is more democratic." Do you agree? Why?

The European Parliament in Strasbourg

Reforming the European Union

Future changes

The **European Union** plans to enlarge. By 2004 it is likely to have an extra ten member states and further enlargements are expected after that. Because of this, the EU needs to be reformed to help it cater for such a large number of member states.

Jack Straw's view

In early 2002, the Foreign Secretary, Jack Straw, published some reforms the UK government would like to see in the European Union. These were designed to make decision-making in Europe faster, more democratic and more effective. Jack Straw was also keen to make it easier for European citizens to understand the work of the EU.

A new European Commission

Along with some other member states, the UK government has agreed that a smaller European Commission is more practical for the future. This could have as few as 12 members. This means that not every country would have its own Commissioner. The smaller states in the EU are concerned about this.

A two-chambered European Parliament?

The UK Government would also like a second chamber in the European Parliament. This would allow for greater scrutiny of new legislation. This second chamber would be made up of MPs from member states. This would allow greater recognition of parliament members by EU citizens.

A cabinet for Europe

The UK would like to see a reduction in the number of specialist councils dealing with different policy areas, such as foreign affairs, agriculture or finance. Each council would elect a President for two-and-a-half years.

The President of each council would then sit on a super council to form a kind of Team Presidency. This council would act like a cabinet for Europe. This super council would then co-ordinate policy across the European Union.

Discuss

Do any of the proposals for change appeal to you? Do you think they might encourage EU citizens to have more interest in the EU? Give examples and reasons for your answers.

Romano Prodi's view

In May 2002, the head of the European Commission, Romano Prodi, published his personal proposals for the future of Europe. They included:

- Encouragement of a Europe-wide citizenship
- A European police force, to police all of the European Union
- Abolition of the national veto, so that all decisions in the Council of Ministers were made by majority voting
- Co-ordination of taxes across the European Union to reduce differences of tax levels between member states

Romano Prodi argued that these proposals were necessary if the European Union was to become an equal partner with the United States. The pressure group, the European Movement argues that we should go further and create a fully Federal Europe, with a directly elected government and directly elected head of state.

Critics of European federalism, including the Conservative party, argue that this is exactly what they feared all along. The Conservatives argue that the European Union should concentrate on enlargement, not more integration.

The budget of the European Union

The Common Agricultural Policy is under discussion.

The European Parliament, together with the Council of Ministers, controls the budget of the European Union, which is set each year.

The European Court of Auditors checks all the revenue and expenditure for the European Union budget, to make sure no fraud is occurring. It also assists the European Parliament in checking the budget each year. There are 15 members of the Court, one per member state. A problem area for the European Court of Auditors has been the Common Agricultural Policy (CAP). This is where member states subsidize farmers to make sure that prices for food remain stable across the EU. The policy has been criticized because it has led to fraud in some states. It is therefore under review as part of future reforms.

The Euro – a single currency

What is the Euro?

The Euro is the **single currency** for 12 member states of the European Union. It was created in January 1999 when 12 states decided to fix their exchange rates for their currencies.

Then, in January 2002, these 12 states introduced the Euro, abolishing their own currencies shortly afterwards. This means that famous old currencies, such as the French franc, the German mark, and the Italian lira, can no longer be used as legal money.

The Euro is a decimal currency. This means it is divided up into units divisible by 10. Each Euro contains 100 cents.

Overseeing the Euro is the European Central Bank. This was set up in Frankfurt in 1998. The role of the Bank is to set interest rates for all countries using the Euro as their national currency. Interest rates help decide the exchange rate – the amount a currency is worth against other currencies. In mid 2002, one Euro was worth £0.64.

Euro coins and notes

The five economic tests

However, three countries – the UK, Denmark, and Sweden have not yet joined the single currency. The position of the UK government has been to see how the single currency works. To evaluate this, the Chancellor, Gordon Brown, has stated there are five economic tests the Euro must pass before the UK could join the single currency. These are:

1 Is the UK economy similar enough to other economies in Europe, so that we and others could live comfortably with euro interest rates on a permanent basis?
2 If problems emerge is there sufficient flexibility in the EU to deal with them?
3 Would joining the euro create better conditions for firms making long-term decisions to invest in Britain?
4 What impact would entry into the euro have on the competitive position of the UK's financial services industry?
5 In summary, will joining the euro promote higher growth, stability and a lasting increase in jobs?

he Government has said that if these tests are passed, it will hold a eferendum and let people within the UK decide whether or not to in the Euro.

Discuss

Do you think the UK should join the single currency? Give reasons.

Imagine you had to design a poster, either for or against the Euro. What message would you use to convince people to agree with you?

Why should we keep the pound?

Groups in favour of keeping the pound include the Conservative Party, the UK Independence Party (UKIP), and the pressure group Europe First. Some Labour backbenchers are also in favour of keeping the pound.

Europe First argues that:

● the economies of member countries may grow or decline in different ways, and at different times
● the Euro would not allow different interest rates to occur, which could lead to one member state going into recession, while another member state experienced economic growth
● the single currency would also lead to inflation. This is because interest rates are lower in the EU than they are in the UK
● introducing the Euro would mean a loss of sovereignty.

Why should we join the Euro?

Groups in favour of the single currency include the Government, the Liberal Democrats and the pressure group, New Europe. They argue that:

● the single currency will create greater economic stability and strength in Europe. Businesses will be able to plan ahead with more certainty
● every time we change a currency, it costs money. With only one currency in Europe, and fewer currency transactions, this would cost less. This would benefit many businesses, and tourists
● interest rates are much lower in Europe. This would mean cheaper mortgages, as interest rates would fall if the UK joined the Euro.

International politics

The decline of the nation state

Countries are sometimes referred to as nation states. For the last 500 years, the nation state has been at the centre of international relations. However, as the world economy has become more global, other institutions have developed. This is so that states can co-operate and debate with each other.

The UK belongs to several other major international institutions. These include the **European Union** (see pages 26–29), the **United Nations** and the **Commonwealth**.

Within the UN

Within the UN, the United Nations Security Council discusses important matters of defence and international security. There are five permanent members of the UN Security Council – the USA, Russia, China, the United Kingdom and France. Each one has a veto. This means that one country can block any motion put before the Security Council. Another 10 countries are temporary members of the Security Council and are elected by the UN General Assembly for two-year terms. The Security Council passes motions by majority vote, unless blocked by a veto.

The United Nations also includes several High Commissions. These deal with matters of international relations, such as refugee and human rights situations.

The United Nations

The United Nations (UN) was set up in 1948, after the Second World War, with the UK as a founding member. It is funded by a contribution from each member country. Currently, there are 189 member countries of the United Nations. Each member country has one vote when passing the decisions of the UN Assembly.

All member countries of the UN sign the UN charter. This commits them to the aims and objectives of the UN, which include:

- maintaining international peace and security
- the protection of human rights
- arms control
- the coordination of aid for refugees and famine victims.

The UN also encourages economic growth and trade between member states.

The United Nations headquarters in New York, USA

Discuss

1 What do you think are the three international issues to which the UN should give top priority?

2 "The UN should be replaced by a world government." Do you agree?

3 Do you think it is fair that each country in the UN has one vote, whatever its size?

The Commonwealth

In the nineteenth century many countries, such as Canada and India, were part of the British Empire. In order to support trade with these countries, the UK set up a 'common wealth' of states. The idea was similar to that of the European Economic Community – to promote free trade within the British Empire. In other words, members of the Commonwealth were able to trade more profitably because they didn't have to pay certain import and export taxes if they traded with other Commonwealth nations.

The Commonwealth still exists today, with the UK sovereign as its head. It is now a voluntary association of 54 countries across the world. These countries meet to discuss economic and international issues, such as globalization, health, education and threats of terrorism.

Supporters of the Commonwealth argue that it gives the United Kingdom an additional international role to play on the world stage. They argue that it is important to maintain the historical links with the countries that were once part of the British Empire. Critics argue that the Commonwealth is outdated and that the UK's real interests ought to lie within Europe.

Discuss

"The Commonwealth is an outdated organisation, and should be disbanded." Discuss this view.

Other political systems

Not all countries in the world are representative democracies. Here are four examples.

Iraq

Iraq has been ruled by Saddam Hussein as a **military dictatorship** since the late 1970s. Unlike a democracy, ordinary citizens have no say in the decision making process. Instead, the head of a military dictatorship has absolute power in that country. This can lead to decisions being made against the wishes of the majority – for example, the use of chemical weapons by Saddam Hussein against Kurds who live in Iraq and oppose him.

addam Hussein in full military uniform

Saudi Arabia

Saudi Arabia has been ruled over by the Saudi royal family for several hundred years. The current ruler of Saudi Arabia is King Fahd. Saudi Arabia is an example of an **absolute monarchy**. This means that all power lies in the hands of the Saudi royal family. All the ministers of the Saudi Arabian government, and all the members of the Cabinet, are members of the royal family.

Saudi Arabia is, therefore, also an example of an **autocracy**. The power wielded by the monarchy is regarded as legitimate, handed on by right of birth through the Saudi royal family.

King Fahd of Saudi Arabia

Cuba

Cuba is a one-party communist state. In other words, only one political party exists – the Communist Party. This used to be the case in the USSR, part of which is now Russia. In 1987, the old communist system fell apart and Russia started to transform into a representative democracy.

Cuba is meant to be a **grassroots democracy**. Debate is meant to occur within branches of the Communist Party on a local level. Ideas are then passed upwards to the national leadership. However, no external opposition is allowed.

This has led the USA to place international **sanctions** against Cuba. Sanctions mean that certain goods are not allowed to be traded between the USA and Cuba. This has made life difficult for ordinary Cubans.

Fidel Castro, the communist leader of Cuba

ran

an is a **theocracy**. In 1979, a revolution overthrew the Shah of Persia, and installed a religious government. Here, members of the majority religion, in this case Islam, make up the parliament, and thus the government. The religious leader in Iran, known as the Ayatollah, wields a great deal of power.

Civil laws are made to conform to the religious teachings of Islam.

Recently, there have been modest reforms in Iran to make it more democratic and to make the government less religious. As a result, present day Iran combines both elements of a theocracy and a democracy.

Discuss

Look at a map of the world. Can you find any other examples of communist countries, absolute monarchies or dictatorships?

Index and Glossary

Absolute monarchy
A hereditary system of government where the ruling family, the monarchy, has total control over a nation state (see page 31).

Autocracy
Government by an individual who is unrestricted by a constitution or laws. A dictatorship is a form of autocracy (see page 31).

Budget
The statement by the government setting out taxes for the year (see pages 16–17).

Cabinet
The 20–25 ministers, appointed by the Prime Minister, who run the government in the UK (see page 3).

Commonwealth
An organisation of countries to promote trade, development and investment between each other (see page 30).

Constituency
An area which elects one MP to the House of Commons (see pages 2, 5–7).

Constitutional monarchy
A system of government with a king or queen as head of state, with limited powers (see page 3).

Councillor
A member of a local government council (see page 25).

County council
The highest level of local government in parts of England (see pages 24–25).

Democracy
A system of government where all the citizens share power (see page 1).

Devolution
A transfer of authority from a central government to regional governments (see pages 10–11).

District council
The lower tier of local government in England (see pages 24–25).

European Union
The 15 countries, including the UK, which have joined together to co-operate on economic and social issues (see pages 26–29).

Executive
The part of the government that makes day-to-day decisions (see page 3).

General election
An election to choose the government, held at least once every five years (see pages 4–5).

Grassroots democracy
A system of government where opinions are gathered at a local level and fed up to the national government (see page 31).

House of Commons
The main (or 'lower') chamber of parliament in the UK (see pages 2, 8–9).

House of Lords
The upper chamber of parliament in the UK (see pages 2, 8, 12–13).

Indirect democracy
See representative democracy (see page 1).

Inflation
The amount the prices of goods have gone up or down over the last 12 months (see pages 16–17).

Judiciary
The part of the government that interprets the law (see page 3).

Law (pl. laws)
A legally binding rule, made to help society work. Laws in the UK are passed by Parliament (see pages 3, 8–9).

Legislature
The part of the government that makes laws (see page 3).

Lobbyist (adj. lobbying)
A professional who tries to influence government decisions (see pages 20, 22).

MEP
A member of the European Parliament (see page 27).

Military dictatorship
A military system of government, where the military has total control over a nation state, through the use or threat of force (see page 31).

MP
A Member of Parliament, that is, of the House of Commons (see pages 2, 4–5, 8–9).

Official Opposition
Usually the second largest party in the House of Commons, whose job is to criticise and 'oppose' the government (see page 3).

Parliament
The legislature of the United Kingdom, where laws are passed (see pages 2–5, 8–9, 12–13).

Peer
A member of the House of Lords (see pages 12–13).

Political party
A collection of local, regional and national people with common interests, who have come together to pursue a common political agenda (see pages 4, 18–19).

Pressure group
A group of people who seek to influence the government, without actually taking power themselves (see pages 20–23).

Prime Minister
The head of the UK government (see pages 3–4, 8–9).

Proportional representation (PR)
A form of electoral system, where the number of seats a party wins is roughly proportional to its national share of the vote (see page 7).

Referendum (pl. referenda)
A special vote to take a particular decision on a particular issue (see page 1).

Representative democracy
A system of government where people elect representatives to make decisions on their behalf. Also known as indirect democracy (see page 1).

Sanctions
An economic ban on the trade of certain goods with a country (see page 31).

Separation of powers
The idea that the legislature, judiciary and executive should be separate from one another (see page 3).

Single currency
The idea that all members of the European Union should share one currency (see pages 18, 29).

Spin doctor
A person who tries to manipulate media coverage (see page 23).

Tax
A percentage of money levied by the government or local council on goods, services or income in order to raise public finances (see pages 16, 25).

Terrorists
People who try to force political change by terrorizing people through murder, violence, and intimidation (see page 20).

Theocracy
A religious system of government, where religious leaders hold power (see page 31).

Trade union
A group of workers in a particular trade who come together to promote their common interests as a pressure group (see pages 2, 21).

Unitary authority
A council that has all the powers of local government (see page 24).

United Nations (UN)
An international organisation of states which promotes peace and co-operation (see page 30).

Westminster
The borough of London that contains the Houses of Parliament, and therefore a term used to refer to central government (see page 8).